The Show Must Go On!

by KRISTIN CASHORE

Editorial Offices: Glenview, Illinois • Parsippany, New Jersey • New York, New York

Sales Offices: Needham, Massachusetts • Duluth, Georgia • Glenview, Illinois
Coppell, Texas • Sacramento, California • Mesa, Arizona

Looking for Fun

People in the United States have always loved entertainment. At the beginning of the 1900s, people all over the country found fun things to do. A family in New York City might spend a day at the amusement parks on Coney Island. A family in Chicago might go to the ballpark to cheer for the local baseball team. Circuses traveled the country by train. People knew they were going to have fun whenever the circus was in town!

In the early 1900s millions of people visited Coney Island in Brooklyn, New York.

The circus was popular in many towns.

The entertainment **industry** in the United States was just beginning to grow. Movies became popular. Broadway musicals became popular first in New York City and spread later to other towns. The radio and the television were invented.

How did entertainment grow and change? One of the first steps toward this growth was called **vaudeville** (VAWD-vill).

Vaudeville

In the early 1900s vaudeville was very popular in the United States. A vaudeville show was a stage show with many short acts. One act usually did not have anything to do with another. For example, a dancing act might come before or after an act with animal tricks. A magic act might come next. Vaudeville shows played in the large cities. They also toured through the small towns.

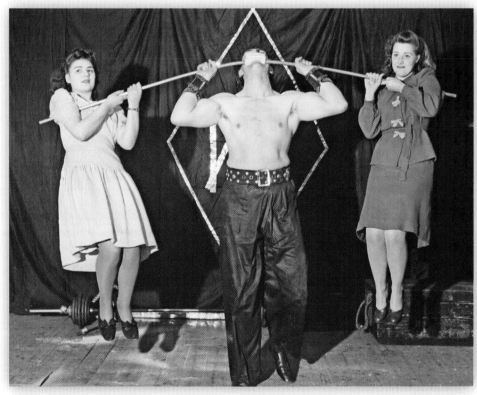

This vaudeville performer is a strong man. He can balance two people with his mouth.

This Broadway theater in New York City featured vaudeville performances.

Vaudeville performers were dancers, singers, and people with special talents. Some vaudeville performers became huge stars. The most famous vaudeville shows took place at the Palace Theater in New York City.

Vaudeville is important in the history of entertainment. Most other kinds of entertainment in the United States grew from vaudeville.

The Movies

During the 1910s and 1920s, movies became popular. The first movies were silent and had no talking or sound effects. Charlie Chaplin and Mary Pickford were big silent movie stars.

Hollywood, California, had nice weather and lots of sunlight. This was a good location for making movies, so Hollywood became the **hub** of moviemaking. Studios, or companies that made movies, became very wealthy. Moviemaking was a very **profitable** business and made a lot of money.

Charlie Chaplin is famous for his silent movies.

The movie *It Happened One Night,* starring Clark Gable and Claudette Colbert, was very popular in 1934.

In the late 1920s inventors figured out how to add sound to movies. The first movies with sound were called "talkies." The movie studios began to make talkies, and audiences loved them! Moviemaking became even more profitable for the studios.

Because movies were so popular, vaudeville began to die out. In 1932 even New York's Palace Theater stopped showing vaudeville. It began to show movies instead.

Radio

In the 1920s radio became popular. The first radio shows were a lot like vaudeville. They had short acts with music or comedy.

By the middle of the 1930s, however, radio had become more like the movies. It was a place for telling stories. There were science fiction radio shows and Westerns. There were mysteries, adventures, and comedies. There were even radio versions of Hollywood movies.

The first radios were very large.

During the 1930s and World War II, President Franklin D. Roosevelt spoke to people over the radio. He talked about what was happening in the country and all around the world.

Radio entertainment became more and more **diverse**. Comedians made audiences laugh. Radio characters, such as the Lone Ranger, the Shadow, and the Green Hornet, stopped crime. Many people listened to soap operas on the radio.

By 1939 about 80 percent of the families in the United States had radios. News was reported live on the radio. President Franklin D. Roosevelt gave radio talks called "fireside chats." Radio connected people with the rest of the world.

Broadway Musicals

Before 1927 most musical shows on Broadway had lots of dancing and singing. Like vaudeville, however, these big productions did not tell much of a story. A **production** is something created with the work of many people and involving many different parts. In 1927 a musical called *Showboat* changed this.

Showboat was a musical play. It had a story line. Its characters had depth. The musical numbers were connected by a plot. *Showboat* told a story.

Showboat changed Broadway musicals. By the 1940s the themes and plots of Broadway musicals were rich. The characters were complicated. Some of the big hits of the 1940s were *Oklahoma!*, *Carousel*, and *South Pacific.*

In 1927 *Showboat* changed Broadway musicals forever.

In the 1930s and 1940s, Fred Astaire and Ginger Rogers danced in Hollywood musicals.

Movie studios in Hollywood also began to make musicals. Singers Judy Garland and Gene Kelly and dancers Fred Astaire and Ginger Rogers lit up the silver screen. Musicals had found their place in American entertainment.

The Movies Meet Television

In the 1940s and 1950s, Hollywood was at its peak. Humphrey Bogart, Katharine Hepburn, and Jimmy Stewart were some of the big stars. A man named Walt Disney began to make animated movies, starting with *Fantasia* in 1940.

In 1941 Orson Welles directed the movie *Citizen Kane.* Just as *Showboat* changed musicals, *Citizen Kane* changed movies. In this movie Welles used photography, sound, editing, and even makeup in new ways. After *Citizen Kane,* movies became more creative.

Citizen Kane changed moviemaking forever.

I Love Lucy was a popular television comedy in the 1950s. It starred actress Lucille Ball (left).

In the 1950s the movies met a challenge: an exciting new invention called television. People no longer had to go to the movies to watch a fun story. They could watch from their own living room!

Comedy shows on television were very popular. Children loved the adventures of a dog named Lassie. Many people enjoyed television soap operas. The news was more interesting because viewers could now watch it live.

People in the United States made television the most popular form of entertainment.

Reaching New Audiences

Today, television, movies, radio, and musicals are still very popular. The entertainment industry is very successful.

Movies, radio, musicals, and television have all changed since their early days. Sometimes they have changed because of new inventions. Other times they have changed because society has changed. Still other times they have changed because they wanted to reach new audiences.

Today, we have many kinds of entertainment to choose from. However, we must not forget the early entertainers. It was the vaudeville shows and silent movies that paved the way for today's movies, radio programs, television shows, and musicals.

Today, the entertainment industry is thriving. People love entertainment!

Glossary

diverse varied

hub a center of activity

industry a business that makes a product or provides a service

production something created with the work of many people and involving many different parts

profitable making a lot of money

vaudeville stage entertainment that involves many short, unrelated acts